PETER PAUPER PRESS
Fine Books and Gifts Since 1928

Our Company

In 1928, at the age of twenty-two, Peter Beilenson began printing books on a small press in the basement of his parents' home in Larchmont, New York. Peter—and later, his wife, Edna—sought to create fine books that sold at "prices even a pauper could afford."

Today, still family owned and operated, Peter Pauper Press continues to honor our founders' legacy of quality, value, and fun for big kids and small kids alike.

ABOUT THE AUTHOR

Born in 1969, **FRÉDÉRIC FURON** studied at the Normandy Schools of Fine Arts and Architecture before turning his attention to history. He currently works as a lecturer and guide for the *Towns and Lands of Art and History* program in Rouen, France—a mecca for the Impressionist movement.

ABOUT THE ILLUSTRATOR

Born in Burgundy in 1977, **FABIEN LAURENT** is a children's book illustrator. He studied design in Nice and at the School of Fine Arts in Toulon, France, then began working as an artist and painter. He shifted his focus exclusively to illustration after winning the prestigious Charles Perreault Award in 2007. Filled with visual humor and tiny details, his storyboards reflect his love of miniatures. Learn more about him at www.fabienlaurent.fr.

First published in the United States by Peter Pauper Press, Inc.
Originally published in France as *Cherche et Trouve: À travers l'art,* © Fleurus Éditions, Paris – 2017. Original French ISBN: 9782215151364

English translation copyright © 2018 by Peter Pauper Press, Inc.
English adaptation by Mady Virgona

Published by Peter Pauper Press, Inc.
202 Mamaroneck Avenue
White Plains, New York 10601 USA

Published in the United Kingdom and Europe by Peter Pauper Press, Inc.
c/o White Pebble International
Unit 2, Plot 11 Terminus Rd.
Chichester, West Sussex PO19 8TX, UK

Library of Congress Cataloging-in-Publication Data

Names: Furon, Frederic, 1969- author. | Laurent, Fabien, 1977- illustrator.
| Virgona, Mady, translator.
Title: Art through the ages / Frederic Furon, Fabien Laurent ; English
adaptation by Mady Virgona.
Other titles: A travers l'art. English
Description: White Plains, New York : Peter Pauper Press, Inc., 2018. |
"Originally published in France as Cherche et Trouve: ?A travers l'art,
Fleurus Editions, Paris, 2017. Original French ISBN: 9782215151364." |
Audience: Age: 7. | Audience: K to Grade 3.
Identifiers: LCCN 2018018339 | ISBN 9781441327994 (hardcover : alk. paper)
Subjects: LCSH: Art--History--Juvenile literature.
Classification: LCC N5308 .F8713 2018 | DDC 700.9--dc23 LC record available at https://lccn.loc.gov/2018018339

ISBN 978-1-4413-2799-4
Manufactured for Peter Pauper Press, Inc.
Printed in China

7 6 5 4 3 2 1
Visit us at www.peterpauper.com

SEEK and FIND

FRÉDÉRIC FURON FABIEN LAURENT

ART THROUGH THE AGES

PETER PAUPER PRESS, INC.
White Plains, New York

PREHISTORY

300,000 BCE — **3,500 BCE**

40,000 BCE
First known art:
Sulawesi cave paintings

35,000 BCE
Chauvet cave paintings

23,000 BCE
Venus of Brassempouy

18,000 BCE
Lascaux cave paintings

ANTIQUITY

3,500 BCE — **476 CE**

2800 BCE
Stonehenge

432 BCE
The
Parthenon

289 BCE
Lighthouse of
Alexandria

Before 79 CE
Frescoes of
Pompeii

80 CE
The Roman
Coliseum

30-400 CE
Fayum mummy
portraits

MIDDLE AGES

476 — **1453**

1145-1240
Chartres Cathedral's
stained glass windows

1066-1082
Bayeux Tapestry

1163-1363
Notre-Dame Cathedral,
Paris

1416
*Très Riches Heures du duc de
Berry* (illuminated manuscript)

1390-1441
Jan van Eyck

RENAISSANCE

1453 — **1640**

1482
Spring, by
Botticelli

1484-1538
*The Lady and
the Unicorn*

1504
David, by
Michelangelo

1506
The *Mona
Lisa*, by
Leonardo
da Vinci

1512
Sistine Chapel
ceiling

1519-1547
King Francis I
and Chambord
Castle

EARLY MODERN PERIOD

1640 — **1789**

1577-1640
Peter Paul Rubens

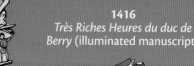
1594-1665
Nicolas Poussin

1660-1715
Louis XIV and
Versailles

CONTEMPORARY PERIOD

1789 — **PRESENT DAY**

1826
The first
photograph

1874
First
Impressionism
show

1890-1910
Art Nouveau

1895
Invention of
moving pictures

1907
Cubism
invented

1910-1935
Art Deco

1924
Surrealism
founded

The 1950s
Pop Art

The 1960s and
beyond
Street Art

**1968 and
beyond**
Land Art

Humans have expressed their creativity since the dawn of time. Throughout history, they have invented new methods to reproduce what they see and express how they feel. We call creative people "artists."

Painting, sculpture, architecture . . . art takes thousands of forms that differ from era to era, and place to place.

Art inspires us to dream and to imagine. By looking at art through the ages, we can also glimpse human history itself—because wherever there is humanity, there is art.

FIND THEM ALL!

ART IS MESSY!

Some great artists from each period, along with their works, are hiding in the crowd in every scene. Try to find them!

A distracted painter has forgotten his palette. Can you spot it in every scene in this book?

ROME WASN'T BUILT IN A DAY
753 BCE TO 476 CE

4

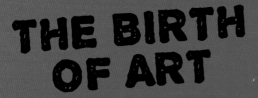

THE BIRTH OF ART

40,000 BCE TO 3,500 BCE

Humans have always wanted to re-create the world around them. The first drawings and sculptures date back to prehistoric times, thousands and thousands of years ago. In caves, we have found animals painted or etched on the walls, sculptures made from clay and stone, and even musical instruments carved from bone. These are the very first recorded works of art.

HOW WAS COLOR CREATED?

Prehistoric artists painted with pigments, which are powders made from animals, plants, or minerals. The most common pigment is ochre, a stone which was ground to create yellows and reds. Charcoal was used to make black paint. The artist would first draw the animal's outline, and then create dimension by blowing pigments onto the image, either directly from their mouth or through a hollow tube.

ANIMALS FROM LONG AGO

Some animals painted onto the walls of prehistoric caves are no longer alive today. Cave lions, cave bears, woolly rhinoceroses, and **mammoths** disappeared thousands of years ago due to weather changes. Some paintings included imaginary half-human, half-animal creatures. Their meaning is lost to us today.

THE HAND GAME

While images of humans are rarely present in the caves, we do see many **painted hands**. These images are called "positive" when the artists covered their hands with paint and then pressed them onto the wall, like a stamp. They are called "negative" when the artists laid their hands on the wall and then painted around them, like a stencil.

3D PREHISTORY

Many **sculptures** show off the talents of prehistoric artists. They used their hands to sculpt figurines out of clay. They also used a piece of sharp flint to carve many other animals from bone, ivory, deer horn, or stone. They would finish their pieces by polishing them until they were smooth to the touch.

THE VENUS OF BRASSEMPOUY

One of the **first human faces in art** was a woman. This small statue was about 1.5 inches (3.8 cm) high and carved from mammoth ivory. Dating back about 25,000 years, this figurine's hair is braided or wavy, and her nose and brow stand out. Her name comes from the area where the carving was found in France.

A MEGALITHIC CIVILIZATION

"Megalithic" comes from the Ancient Greek words *mega*, meaning "great," and *lithos*, meaning "stone." Toward the end of the Prehistoric period, humans built large stone structures, which we now call **megaliths**. The purpose of megaliths is still shrouded in mystery today, but they related to the sun, the seasons, and most likely to early agriculture.

FIND THEM ALL!

THE REAL ANTIQUES!

2,000 BCE TO 27 BCE

Ancient Greek art was extremely important in Europe. Between 450 BCE and 320 BCE, its cultural influence spread from Egypt to India and into the Middle East. For centuries, artists were inspired by Greek stories and myths, such as tales from the Trojan War or the adventures of Ulysses. Today, art-lovers visit museums all around the world to marvel at masterpieces by Greek painters and sculptors.

GODDESSES OF ART

A building that houses art collections is known as a "museum." This word comes from the **Muses**, nine goddesses who were thought to inspire all artists. Each Muse guides a different art form—from poetry to dance and from music to theater—as well as history and astronomy.

PAINTING ON CLAY

The Greeks made beautiful **pottery** that was traded all over the Mediterranean, and became famous far and wide. They painted scenes on their ceramics, often illustrating stories from mythology. Most featured black artwork on a red background, or red artwork on a black background.

IN THE NAME OF THE GODS

The Greeks built many temples to worship their gods. Made of sparkling white marble and painted in vivid colors, most were decorated with carved scenes from the lives of Greek gods and goddesses. The **Parthenon** in Athens, which is dedicated to the goddess Athena, is the most famous of these temples still standing today.

TITANIC STATUES

Phidias was a Greek sculptor famous for his "chryselephantine" statues, created with gold (*chrysos* in Greek) and ivory (*elephas* in Greek). Nearly 40 feet (12 m) high, his statue of Zeus, God of the Sky, was located in a huge temple at Olympia. Though it was destroyed long ago, the statue was one of the Seven Wonders of the Ancient World.

LIGHTING THE WORLD

The **Great Lighthouse of Alexandria**, in Egypt, was designed by the Greeks in 290 BCE. Also considered one of the Seven Wonders of the Ancient World, it was nearly 450 feet (137 m) high, and guided sailors into port. After a series of earthquakes, it crumbled into the sea around 1300 CE.

CREATING A BRONZE STATUE

The Greeks crafted many statues using the **lost-wax technique**. First, they created a wax model and covered it in clay. The sculptor then poked small holes in the clay, and put the piece in an oven. The oven's heat caused the wax to melt and flow out through the holes. Next, liquid bronze was poured into the clay mold. The bronze cooled and hardened. Finally, the clay was cracked open to reveal the bronze statue.

ROME WASN'T BUILT IN A DAY

753 BCE TO 476 CE

Between 202 BCE and 476 CE, the Roman Empire ruled large areas of Europe and the Mediterranean basin. Through military conquests and trade, the Romans imported beautiful materials like marble into their capital, and made them into splendid buildings and art. True art-lovers, the Romans also decorated their fancy villas with pilfered Greek artwork. Their architectural style inspired many buildings throughout history.

INFLUENTIAL NEIGHBORS

At first, the Romans imitated many Greek art forms and produced their own copies, whose quality was often not very good. They were also influenced by the **Etruscans**, a nearby people with outstanding sculptors and silversmiths (jewelry makers). Wealthy Etruscan families, from which the first kings of Rome were born, also commissioned ornate tombstones.

GREAT MASTERPIECES FROM SMALL STONES

Romans especially liked **mosaics**. Tiny colored stones were cut into cubes called *tesserae* and then glued together in patterns or shapes. The finished mosaics often decorated floors or walls. Mosaic art depicted everything from daily Roman life, to animals, to battles.

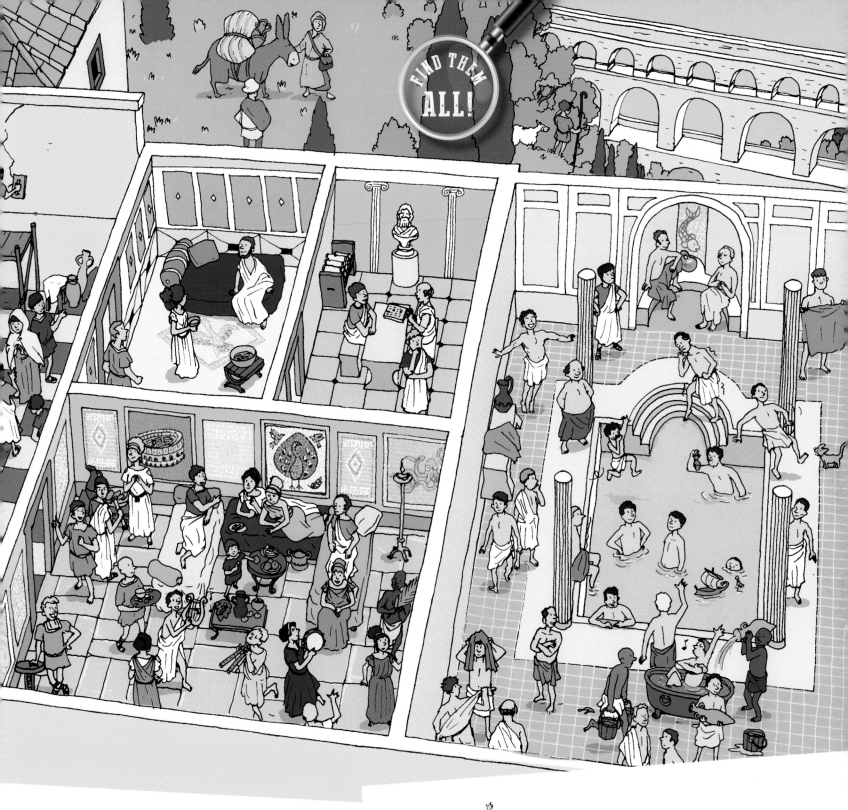

NO WALLPAPER ALLOWED!

Romans also covered the walls of their villas with stucco, a plaster made from limestone. After being heated to a high temperature and finely crushed, the powder was mixed with water, sand, glue, and sometimes marble dust. Sometimes color was also added. Next, the plaster was painted while it was still damp. A painting on wet plaster is called a **fresco** (from the Italian word *fresco*, meaning "fresh").

LEGENDARY BUILDERS

The Romans were brilliant architects. Throughout their Empire, they built theaters, circuses where people would come to see chariot races, aqueducts to transport water, and huge temples. In Rome, you can still admire the **Coliseum**, a stadium where gladiator battles were held, and the Pantheon, a temple topped by a gigantic concrete dome!

WATER, WATER EVERYWHERE!

Bathing was very important to the Romans, both to stay clean and because they enjoyed it. Their public baths, or **thermae**, were luxuriously decorated. The Baths of the Emperor Caracalla are completely covered in marble, gilt bronze, mosaics, and giant statues weighing as much as 24 tons!

PORTRAIT ART

A series of **painted sarcophagi** (or coffins) were discovered in the Fayum region of Egypt, which the Romans had conquered. The dead look as though they are posing. With their strong brushstrokes and brilliant colors, these portraits are very realistic. They depict these people as though they were still alive—including the twinkle in their eyes! The mummy paintings are considered a unique art form.

THE TIME OF CATHEDRALS

476 TO 1453

After the Roman Empire came the Middle Ages, a period that lasted nearly one thousand years! Medieval art is mainly religious and celebrates the power of the Christian Church, which became the dominant religion across nearly all of Europe. Artists created interpretations of Bible stories and of the lives of martyrs and saints. These can be seen on the façades of cathedrals and homes, in early books and manuscripts, on stained glass, and in paintings.

HEAVENLY CATHEDRALS

Since they were meant to portray all of Heaven's glory, cathedrals were luxuriously decorated with statues, frescoes, tapestries, wood carvings, and golden altars. Sunlight shone through beautiful **stained-glass windows**, created by assembling colored glass pieces into a frame made from molten lead pieces. When light came through the windows, their many colors were projected onto the cathedral walls.

WHAT'S AN ARTIST?

The word *artist* did not exist in the Middle Ages. Instead, sculptors and painters were considered artisans or craftsmen. A statue sculptor was called an **imagist** because he created pictures with stone. Our concept of art has evolved over time. Things we consider artistic today were not always thought of as art.

SACRED IMAGES

The Middle Ages also saw the beginnings of **books** as we know them today. Considered luxury items, the first books contained sacred works, and were hand-illustrated by copyist monks. Later, books explored other topics, such as hunting. These books were painted with tiny, incredibly detailed scenes, or "illuminations," filled with animals, flowers, and intricate designs.

A WORLD OF COLOR

In the Middle Ages, people prized color not only for its beauty, but also because it showed off the wealth of the person wearing it. Certain bright pigments were very rare, and things containing those colors cost a lot. Color was also used as a code in art. For example, artists show the Virgin Mary wearing a blue coat, because it is the color of the sky. In contrast, an **executioner** was often shown wearing red—the color of blood.

SHOWING DEVOTION

Some works of art, especially statues carved from stone or wood, were covered in jewels or gold leaf. Religious people would travel long distances to see them. They usually contained a **relic**: a bone or small piece of clothing from a saint. Relics were thought to have magical powers that would heal and protect.

STORIES IN ART

The Church spread its teachings through ornate sculptures and paintings that illustrated stories from the Bible and the lives of the saints, while dazzling with their beauty. Churches displayed scenes from religious stories on the tympanum above the cathedral doors, and on the **altarpieces**, large paintings made up of several wooden panels and placed behind the altar.

THE RENAISSANCE: LOOKING TO THE PAST

1400 TO 1500

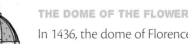

THE DOME OF THE FLOWER

In 1436, the dome of Florence's great cathedral, **Santa Maria del Fiore** (Italian for "Saint Mary of the Flower"), became the largest ever created. Soaring over 350 feet (107 m) high, nearly 150 feet (45.4 m) in diameter, and weighing over 37,000 tons, the Dome was the greatest technical and artistic challenge of its time. It was designed by architect Filippo Brunelleschi and built from a double brick shell.

SPRING HAS SPRUNG!

Spring by Sandro Botticelli is one of the most famous paintings of the Italian Renaissance. The people in it are allegories from mythology, which means they are representations of ideas in human form. The painter depicts flowers, love, and the wind, as well as qualities like grace and beauty.

Through trade, many towns in Northern Italy and Flanders (north of France) became rich. A strong rivalry developed between them, and each competed to become the most beautiful and wealthiest place in Europe. While archaeologists started digging up the ruins of ancient Rome in the 1440s, a new school of philosophy and art, humanism, began to spread. Ancient Greek and Roman art became popular again. Artists flocked to these cities, and were hired to create works celebrating their famous and wealthy patrons.

THREE ARTISTS, ONE KING

Biblical texts also provided powerful artistic inspiration during the Middle Ages. As a result, three great artists—**Donatello** in 1440, **Verrocchio** in 1475, and **Michelangelo** in 1504—created unique images of David, a young shepherd. In a biblical story, before becoming the King of Israel, David used his slingshot to defeat Goliath, the giant.

A UNIVERSAL GENIUS

Leonardo da Vinci's fame has never waned through the centuries. Even today, people see him as the spirit of the Renaissance. A student of Verrocchio, he was an accomplished artist whose talent led him to explore every scientific and artistic field of his time. Leonardo also created the world's most famous painting, the *Mona Lisa*.

PAINTING ON CLOTH

While the earliest known **painting on linen** dates back to 1410, this new method spread far and wide during the Renaissance. Before, artists used wood panels glued together and then coated in plaster. Techniques were also changing: artists slowly moved away from tempera paint—where egg yolk and water are used to bind the pigment—and toward oil-based paints.

THE SISTINE CHAPEL

Some religious leaders thought the subjects painted and sculpted by Renaissance artists were immoral, and condemned them. This did not stop the Church from commissioning works from the most talented painters and sculptors. Michelangelo was hired to paint frescoes on the ceiling of the Sistine Chapel in the Roman Vatican, where the Pope lives. Among the most famous of these frescoes is ***The Creation of Adam.***

FIND THEM ALL!

AT THE COURT OF KINGS

1498 TO 1610

Kings and queens surrounded themselves with impressive courts, attracting top artists to work for them. Huge sums of money were spent on art that glorified monarchs, and through them, the countries they ruled. Palaces were filled with furniture made from rare and precious materials, their walls covered in shimmering tapestries and paintings that showed the king as superior to everyone. Artists could not refuse a chance to work at court, as competition was fierce and such jobs were rare.

FANCY MANSIONS

 In the 16th Century, the King of France and his court had no permanent home, so many *châteaux* (palaces) flourished along the Loire River and south of Paris. There, King Francis I invited famous Italian artists to build the crown jewel of his court. Painter and architect Le Primatrice developed the setting for Fontainebleau Palace, while Leonardo da Vinci created the first blueprints for the **Chambord Castle**.

KINGS AND RIVALS

 Sometimes, a talented and successful artist got the chance to become Painter to the King, and to paint the King's portrait. Two artists were especially admired for creating portraits that really looked like their subjects: François Clouet at the court of **Francis I** of France, and Hans Holbein at the court of **Henry VIII** of England.

POTTERY THAT GLOWS

 A true jack of all trades, Bernard Palissy was a potter, painter, enameler, and glassmaker as well as a scientist. He is known for his **ceramic plates** decorated with realistic images of fish, eels, and plants. A hard worker, Palissy would even throw his own furniture into his ovens to keep the fires burning for his art!

THREADS AND FINERY

 The nobility's manors were filled with multicolored tapestries. Carefully crafted, they illustrate hunting scenes, stories from mythology, or philosophical concepts. One example is the **Lady and the Unicorn**, a series of tapestries woven around 1500 that depict the five senses: taste, smell, sight, hearing, and touch.

MASTER ENGRAVER

 The art of engraving appeared in Europe shortly after the printing press arrived, in the early days of books. Used in Asia since the Middle Ages, this process involves carving an image onto a block of wood, coating its surface with ink, and then applying it onto paper, like a stamp. German artist **Albrecht Dürer** is especially famous for his engravings.

FOR ETERNITY AND BEYOND!

 Monarchs wanted to make sure they and their many achievements would be remembered after their deaths, so they built **lavish tombs and monuments**. Colored marble, bronze, sculpture—every material and technique was used to ensure their memory would live on for eternity. Some tombs even had two levels, with the living king's statue on top, and the deceased king's likeness on the lower level.

AROUND THE ACADEMY

1648 TO 1750

Founded in France in 1648, the Royal Academy of Painting and Sculpture was created to encourage art, but also to control it. By following strict rules inspired by ancient Greece and Rome, artists would produce beautiful works that upheld particular values. This artistic philosophy is known as Classicism. Classicism valued reason, and was opposed by a different movement, Baroque, which valued passion. The tension between these two movements led to one of the richest periods in Western art history.

A PEARL OF AN ART FORM

Baroque is an art style with swirling shapes, grand movements, and bright colors. Strong feelings are highlighted, even when they are negative or overly dramatic. The word "baroque" comes from *barocco*, a Portuguese term for an irregular, shimmering **pearl** sometimes found in oysters.

PETER PAUL RUBENS

The baroque style of Peter Paul Rubens can be seen in the bold, twisting bodies and flowing curves of his subjects. Color is especially important in his work, to the point where it can overshadow the subjects themselves. Both a celebrated painter and an ambassador, Rubens was one of the most influential artists of his time. Many of his pieces were commissioned by **Marie de' Medici**, the Queen of France.

VISUALIZING THE SPACE

Before they began their paintings, painters would often create **cardboard models** on a grid. Next, the painters would prepare wax figurines of the people they wanted to paint, dress them, and move them around inside the models until they got everything just right. By starting with a model, painters could better understand the spaces they painted.

AN ANCIENT STATUE

The statue **Laocoön and His Sons** is made of several large marble blocks. Lost for centuries, it was rediscovered in Rome in 1506. Baroque artists were deeply moved and impressed by the tensed muscles and realistic expressions of its subjects, and were often inspired to imitate them.

A KING'S DREAM

Many believe the Palace of Versailles is the best example of classicism. Its outside is inspired by Roman temples, and its proportions look beautifully balanced. Made into a palace by **Louis XIV**, Versailles was designed to showcase the king himself. Its main architects were Louis Le Vau and Jules Hardouin-Mansart.

THE GREAT POUSSIN

Nicolas Poussin is considered one of the best classical painters. Inspired by mythological and biblical stories, Poussin arranged his paintings with clear, geometric precision. To emphasize the harmony of his shapes, he used smooth paint, almost invisible brushstrokes, and soft, luminous colors.

FIND THEM ALL!

MOVING TOWARD NEW FORMS
1840 TO 1900

Between 1840 and 1860, more and more voices began to complain against the Academy's domination over art. Some young students, who didn't like the sameness of the Academy's styles, developed new ways of representing the world. The society of the time was reluctant to change, and tried its best to stop this new movement. However, in only thirty to forty years, a true revolution took place—one that permanently changed old ideas about art.

IMPRESSION, SUNRISE

Together, the painters **Claude Monet**, Auguste Renoir, Frédéric Bazille, and Alfred Sisley created a movement called Impressionism. The name came from an 1872 painting by Monet entitled *Impression, Sunrise*. A huge scandal erupted during their first group exhibition. For the first time in Western art history, color became more important than precision in a painting.

SPLOTCHES

In 1839, a chemist named **Chevreul** published a book explaining that the brain itself can create color. If you place two splotches of color—one yellow and one red—side by side, and then step farther and farther away, the two colors gradually merge to form only one color—orange. This is the same technique used by the Impressionists, as their brushstrokes on the canvas reveal.

CAPTURING A MOMENT

Photography first appeared between 1826 and 1839. This new art form, which captures an image exactly as it appears, was soon used for creative purposes. Staged photos depicting historical or literary subjects began to appear. Early photo-montages (or images made out of several photographs) also showed wondrous scenes, and were very popular.

SCULPTURES

What the Impressionists were doing with paint, **Camille Claudel** and **Auguste Rodin** were doing with sculpture. These two talented artists had a complex relationship filled with admiration, love, and rivalry. Through the strength and power of their pieces, they became two of the most influential, original sculptors of their time.

MORE AND MORE COLOR!

Originally an Impressionist, **Paul Gauguin** traveled all over, and spent many years in Tahiti, an island whose light and color he loved to paint. With their bold lines and large areas of vivid color—a bit like stained glass—his paintings would strongly influence the next generation of artists.

NEW TECHNOLOGIES

For a long time, painters rarely left their studios. Painting materials were heavy and beautiful landscapes were far from the cities where they lived. The development of the railroad, and new inventions like the portable easel and the **paint tube**, made it much easier for artists to travel and paint new scenery.

MODERN LIGHTS

1900 TO 1950

After the shock created by the Impressionists, the Academy gave way to novelty, and every artistic field opened to previously unimaginable new horizons. As Europe alternated between brief periods of peace and two world wars, new art forms and styles blossomed. Vienna, Paris, and Berlin became artistic capitals. Each city attracted a thousand and one artists inspired by modern events.

THE ART OF NOODLES

Art Nouveau is a movement that appeared in northern Europe near the end of the 1800s. Filled with lean, curved, and twisting shapes, it was quickly nicknamed "noodle art" in France. Art Nouveau can be found in virtually all art forms, from furniture to architecture and from painting to jewelry.

A BOX FULL OF PERSPECTIVE

Two painters living in Paris, **Pablo Picasso** and Georges Braque, invented Cubism in 1907. The world had never seen such a scandal! Some even said that this was the end of art itself! In fact, it was simply another way of seeing the world—an attempt to show an object from several different angles at the same time.

MOVING IMAGES

Cinema was invented by the Lumière brothers in 1895. Soon after, this curiosity would earn recognition as a full-fledged art form. Cinema was excellent for creating a sense of wonder. Talented artists such as **Méliès** (*A Trip to the Moon*) and Cocteau (*Beauty and the Beast*) used film to present their poetic visions.

THE MASTERS OF MODERNITY

Along with Picasso, some call **Henri Matisse** the most influential Western painter of this time. He was the master of Fauvism, a movement inspired by Gauguin and others. Matisse used unmixed, vivid areas of color known as "flats" to cover large parts of his canvases. It didn't matter if the sky was yellow or purple . . . so long as it was brightly colored!

BEYOND REALITY

In their quest for new excitement, artists wanted to break free of logic and express their thoughts. They created strange shapes from their imagination. Some shapes didn't represent any real things; this is called abstraction. Others like **Salvador Dali**, with his painted world of flaming giraffes and melting clocks, presented an extreme view of reality. This is known as Surrealism.

REACHING FOR THE SKY

Reinforced concrete is made from concrete and steel rods. Used for the first time around 1892, it started a revolution in architecture. Buildings could take shapes that had been impossible before, and achieve incredible heights. The first skyscrapers were born. **The Chrysler Building**, in New York City, is one of the jewels of the Art Deco movement.

FIND THEM ALL!

Le Bistr

POP ART!

1950 TO 1970

World War II ended in 1945. After a period of great suffering, the West began to recover. Artists looked to the future and continued to challenge the meaning of art, a process that had started fifty years earlier. Two movements emerged at the same time. One returned to figurative art, or showing things in recognizable forms. The other leaned toward abstraction, or presenting things in ways that capture the imagination.

POP ART

Born in England, the **pop art** movement came to the United States, where many artists had fled during the war. An abbreviation of "popular art," this movement presented common objects as works of art, far away from their usual use. Comic books and advertisements became a source of inspiration.

WARHOL AND HIS GANG

The artist **Andy Warhol** lived in New York, where he first displayed his work in 1952. His interest in things people bought in stores was inspired by his work in advertising. He created many artwork series, such as portraits of famous actors in super-bright colors. Famous people mingled at his workshop, known as The Factory.

FULL-BODY PAINTING

American abstract artist **Jackson Pollock** created a unique form of "action painting." After laying a canvas on the floor, he used a stick or knife to throw paint onto it with big, energetic movements. The artist's body came alive, like a dancer, and a variety of different patterns and designs emerged.

THE NEW REALISTS

In France, artists also wanted to return to realism, with art that showed objects outside of their main uses. Arman showed a box filled with dentures (false teeth) that he called "A Bite out of Life," and **Jean Tinguely** put together sculpture-like machines covered in useless gears. César created sculptures out of squashed and crushed items, including the French cinema award named after him.

EVEN MORE COLOR

Mark Rothko's abstract paintings focus completely on color. Freed from the need for a subject, they are made up of large patches of vibrant color with blurred edges. The simplicity of these pieces inspires calm and contemplation.

AERIAL ARCHITECTURE

As technology made new kinds of buildings possible, people turned their eyes to the sky. **Graceful, rounded architectural shapes** inspired by science fiction and our vision of the future emerged.

SO, WHAT'S NEXT?

Like the civilizations that gave rise to it, art continues to evolve. It has taken thousands of different forms over the centuries, adapting to people's interests and values, and to new technologies. Of course, some art is in museums, and will always be a part of history. But art is also being created right now, all around us, looking for new ways to surprise and delight. Trying to define art, once and for all, is like trying to catch a bird in flight with your bare hands.

THERE'S AN IDEA!

The definition of art has expanded further still. Today, artists exhibit **installations**, which are sets of unexpected or surprising objects intended to make us question our way of life. When the artist's statement, which discusses the installation, becomes more important than the installation itself, this is known as conceptual art.

BACK TO NATURE

Some sculptors are turning back to nature and its landscapes, far from the noise of the city. Temporary or permanent works are laid out in a specific way, in a location carefully chosen by the artist. Their purpose is to raise questions or generate a sense of harmony or wonder. The artist uses sand, wood, stone, and other natural materials. This is known as **land art**.

STREET ART

Artists in cities sometimes install their artwork right in the street, or in abandoned buildings. Painted on walls or free-standing, the art surprises people as they walk by. These pieces may be political, condemn social inequality and wrongs, or inspire viewers to daydream. This is called **street art**.

CREATING THE IMPOSSIBLE

Today, architects use computers to plan their buildings, which allows them to be even more daring in their creations. Around the world, buildings are covered in plants or shaped like a ship's sail. In Singapore, colossal lighted "**supertrees**" dwarf the landscape. These works, which could only be imagined in the past, have become a reality today.

MOVING TOWARD A VIRTUAL WORLD

As **information technology** and networks continue to grow, the world is also changing. The boundaries of reality are gradually fading away. Some computer-generated movies, photos, and paintings may be more lifelike than reality itself! Artists are happily using these new modes of expression for their work.

LIMITLESS

Newness always creates curiosity, along with some fear. The same is true for every new art form. Some works are considered scandalous because they raise questions about what can be said or shown, and where. For example, some people strongly criticized **Jeff Koons' giant balloon animals** when they were exhibited at the Palace of Versailles.

Did you find everything on the Seek and Find pages? Try this extra challenge! The following people, objects, and works of art are hidden throughout this book. If you get stumped, try using what you've learned about each time period and art movement.